A Kid's Guide to Planting, Growing, and Preparing Food

Garden to Table

WITH CHEF-IN-RESIDENCE LISA WAGNER

SCARLETTA **JUNIOR READERS**

MINNEAPOLIS, MINNESOTA

The Lexile Framework for Reading®
Lexile Measure® 620L
LEXILE®, LEXILE FRAMEWORK®, LEXILE ANALYZER® and the LEXILE® logo are trademarks of MetaMetrics, Inc., and are registered in the United States and abroad. The trademarks and names of other companies and products mentioned herein are the property of their respective owners. Copyright © 2011 MetaMetrics, Inc. All rights reserved.

Library of Congress Cataloging-in-Publication Data
Hengel, Katherine.
 Garden to table : a kid's guide to planting, growing, and preparing food / by Katherine Hengel.
   pages cm
Includes bibliographical references and index.
Audience: Ages 8-12.
Audience: Grades 4 to 6.
ISBN 978-1-938063-42-8 (pbk.) -- ISBN 978-1-938063-43-5 (electronic)
1. Cooking--Juvenile literature. 2. Vegetable gardening--Juvenile literature. I. Title.
TX652.5.H454 2014
641.5--dc23
            2013037309

Interior Design and Production: Anders Hanson, Mighty Media, Inc., Minneapolis, MN
Cover Design: Colleen Dolphin
Editor: Josh Plattner
Photo credits: Aaron DeYoe, Shutterstock. Photos on page 5 courtesy of W. Atlee Burpee & Co. and Kitazawa Seed Co.

The following manufacturers/names appearing in this book are trademarks:
Argo®, Arm & Hammer®, A Taste of Thai®, Barilla®, Chefmate®, Crystal Sugar®, E-Z Foil®, Galbani®, Gedney®, Gold Medal Flour®, Heinz®, Hellman's®, Hidden Valley®, Hormel™, Inglehoffer®, International Collection™, Kemps®, Kerr®, Kitchen Aid®, Kraft®, Land O'Lakes®, Market Pantry®, Marukan®, McCormick®, Michael Graves Design®, Pam®, Pompeii®, Proctor Silex®, Progresso®, Pyrex®, Roundy's®, The Pampered Chef®, Zatarain's®

Distributed by Publishers Group West
Printed and manufactured in the United States
North Mankato, Minnesota

 PRINTED ON RECYCLED PAPER

Safety First!

Some recipes call for activities or ingredients that require caution. If you see these symbols, ask an adult for help!

Sharp - *You need to use a sharp knife or cutting tool for this recipe.*

Hot - *This recipe requires handling hot objects. Always use oven mitts when holding hot pans.*

Nuts - *This recipe includes nuts. People with nut allergies should not eat it.*

CONTENTS

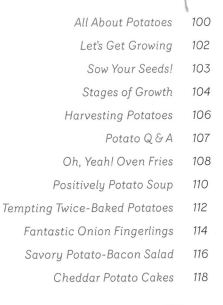

WHY GROW YOUR OWN FOOD?

Because then you get to eat it, of course! You might not be the biggest vegetable fan in the world. But have you ever had fresh produce? Straight from your very own garden? If not, prepare to be surprised. Fresh food tastes wonderful!

Plus, fresh food is really healthy. All produce is good for you. But produce that comes from your own garden is the very best. Most folks do not use chemicals in their home gardens. That makes home gardens better for you and the **environment**!

Growing your own food is rewarding. All it takes is time, patience, soil, water, and sunshine! This book will teach you how to grow basil in **containers**. Once it's ready, we're going to use it in some tasty recipes!

Cooking Terms

Boil

Boil means to heat liquid until it begins to bubble.

Arrange

Arrange means to place things in a certain order or pattern.

Beat

Beat means to mix well using a whisk or electric mixer.

Brush

Brush means to spread a liquid on something using a basting brush.

Chop

Chop means to cut into small pieces.

Coat

Coat means to cover something with another ingredient or mixture.

Cube

Cube means to cut something into small squares with a knife.

Dice

Dice means to cut something into small squares with a knife.

Drain

Drain means to remove liquid using a strainer or colander.

Drizzle

Drizzle means to slowly pour a liquid over something.

Cooking Terms

Fold

Fold means to mix ingredients by gently lifting and turning.

Fluff

Fluff means to loosen or separate using a fork.

Grate

Grate means to shred something into small pieces using a grater.

Grease

Grease means to coat something with butter or oil.

Julienne

Julienne means to slice into very thin strips.

Mash

Mash means to press down and smash food with a fork or potato masher.

Peel

Peel means to remove the skin, often with a peeler.

Press

Press means to push an ingredient, often garlic through a garlic press.

LENGTHWISE OR CROSSWISE

To cut something lengthwise means to cut along its length. You create pieces that are the same length as the original.

To cut something crosswise means to cut across its length. The pieces will be shorter, but the same width as the original.

Cooking Terms

Roll

Roll means to wrap something around itself into a tube.

Slice

Slice means to cut food into pieces of the same thickness.

Spread

Spread means to make a smooth layer with a spoon, knife, or spatula.

Stir-Fry

Stir-fry means to fry quickly over high heat in an oiled pan while stirring continuously.

Toast

Toast means to cook something until the outside is brown and crispy.

Toss

Toss means to turn ingredients over to coat them with seasonings.

Whisk

Whisk means to beat quickly by hand with a whisk or a fork.

Zest

Zest means to lightly remove some of the peel from a citrus fruit using a zester.

SHREDDING LETTUCE

Some recipes call for shredded lettuce. To shred lettuce, put several clean leaves that are about the same size on top of each other. Roll them up. Then slice crosswise. Cut ¼ inch (.5 cm) off at a time. To cut something crosswise means to cut across its length. The pieces will be shorter, but the same width as the original.

Cool Ingredients

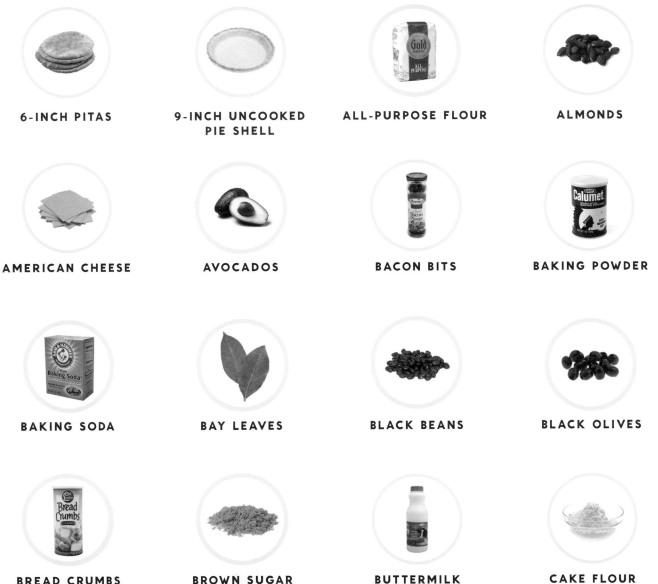

6-INCH PITAS

9-INCH UNCOOKED PIE SHELL

ALL-PURPOSE FLOUR

ALMONDS

AMERICAN CHEESE

AVOCADOS

BACON BITS

BAKING POWDER

BAKING SODA

BAY LEAVES

BLACK BEANS

BLACK OLIVES

BREAD CRUMBS

BROWN SUGAR

BUTTERMILK

CAKE FLOUR

CANNED CORN

CANNED TOMATOES

CARROTS

CASHEWS

CAYENNE PEPPER

CHEDDAR CHEESE

CHERRY TOMATOES

CHICKEN BROTH

CHIVES

CIDER VINEGAR

COLBY CHEESE

CORNSTARCH

CRUMBLED BLUE CHEESE

CRUSHED RED PEPPER FLAKES

CUCUMBER

CUMIN

Cool Ingredients

DICED HAM

DIJON MUSTARD

FENNEL SEEDS

FETTUCCINE

FISH SAUCE

FLOUR TORTILLAS

FRESH BASIL

FRESH BEAN SPROUTS

FRESH CILANTRO

FRESH DILL

GARLIC CLOVES

GOLDEN RAISINS

GREEN ONIONS

GROUND CINNAMON

HALF-AND-HALF

HAM BONE

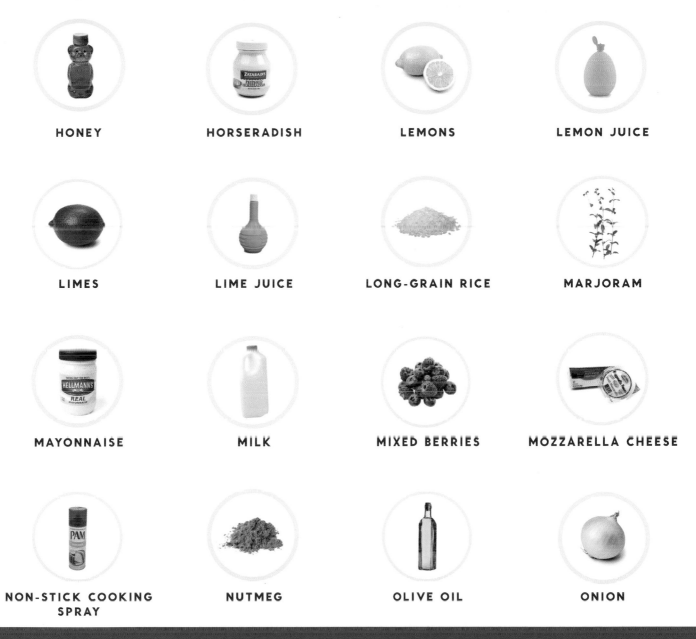

HONEY

HORSERADISH

LEMONS

LEMON JUICE

LIMES

LIME JUICE

LONG-GRAIN RICE

MARJORAM

MAYONNAISE

MILK

MIXED BERRIES

MOZZARELLA CHEESE

NON-STICK COOKING SPRAY

NUTMEG

OLIVE OIL

ONION

Cool Ingredients

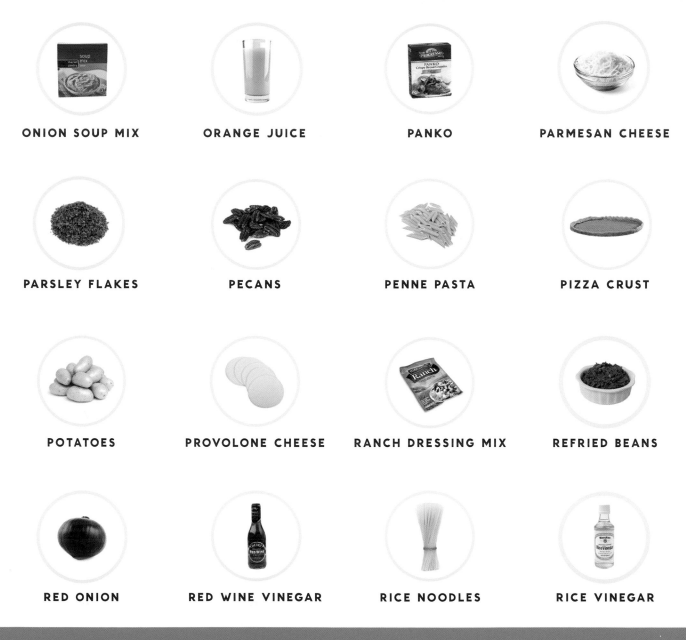

ONION SOUP MIX

ORANGE JUICE

PANKO

PARMESAN CHEESE

PARSLEY FLAKES

PECANS

PENNE PASTA

PIZZA CRUST

POTATOES

PROVOLONE CHEESE

RANCH DRESSING MIX

REFRIED BEANS

RED ONION

RED WINE VINEGAR

RICE NOODLES

RICE VINEGAR

Some people are **allergic** to certain foods. This means they can get very sick if they eat them. They might need **emergency** medical help. Nut allergies are serious and can be especially harmful. Before you serve anything made with nuts or peanut oil, ask if anyone has a nut allergy.

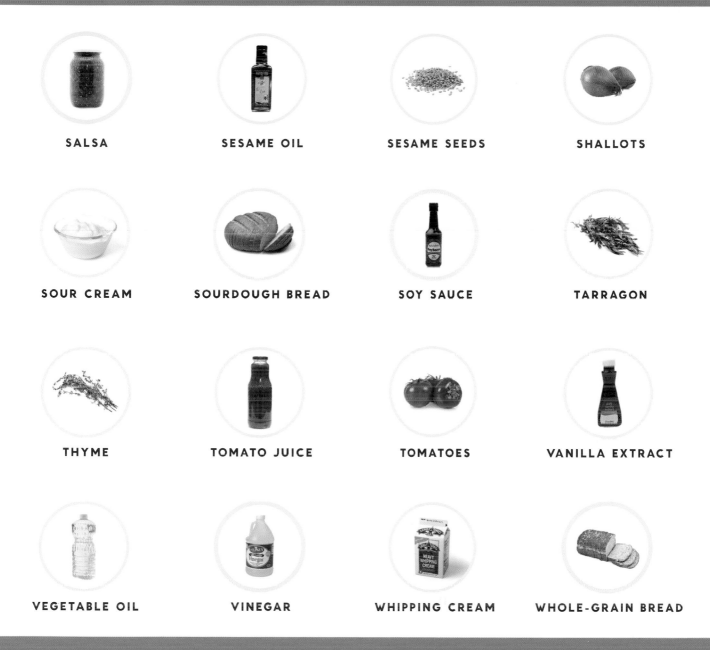

SALSA	**SESAME OIL**	**SESAME SEEDS**	**SHALLOTS**
SOUR CREAM	**SOURDOUGH BREAD**	**SOY SAUCE**	**TARRAGON**
THYME	**TOMATO JUICE**	**TOMATOES**	**VANILLA EXTRACT**
VEGETABLE OIL	**VINEGAR**	**WHIPPING CREAM**	**WHOLE-GRAIN BREAD**

Kitchen Tools

8×8-INCH BAKING DISH

9X9-INCH BAKING DISH

9-INCH SPRINGFORM PAN

12-MUFFIN TIN

ALUMINUM FOIL

BAKING SHEET

BASTING BRUSH

BLENDER

BREAD KNIFE

CAN OPENER

CUTTING BOARD

DINNER KNIFE

FRYING PAN WITH LID

FUNNEL

HAND MIXER

GARLIC PRESS

GRATER

JAR WITH A LID

KITCHEN SCISSORS

LADLE

LARGE POT WITH LID

MEASURING CUPS

MEASURING SPOONS

MEDIUM POT

Kitchen Tools

MIXING BOWLS

MIXING SPOON

NON-STICK FRYING PAN

OVEN MITTS

OVEN-SAFE GLASS BOWLS

PAPER LINERS

PAPER TOWELS

PASTA SERVER

PEELER

PIE PAN

PINT JAR WITH COVER

PLASTIC WRAP

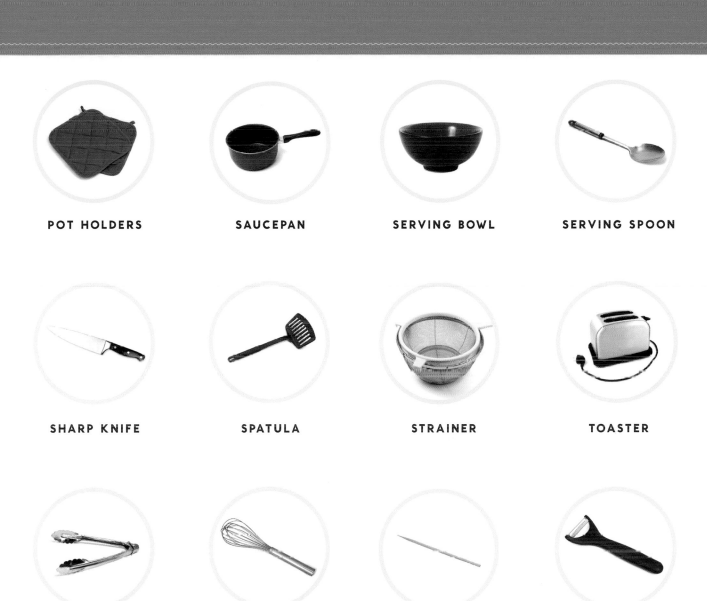

POT HOLDERS

SAUCEPAN

SERVING BOWL

SERVING SPOON

SHARP KNIFE

SPATULA

STRAINER

TOASTER

TONGS

WHISK

WOODEN TOOTHPICK

ZESTER

ALL ABOUT
BASIL

Basil is a tender **herb** that grows low to the ground. It originated in India and Iran. It has been around for thousands of years.

There are several kinds of basil. Italian dishes often call for sweet basil. Thai basil, lemon basil, and holy basil are frequently used in Asian dishes. Basil's flavor changes when it is cooked. So it is usually used fresh.

In this section, we're going to grow and cook sweet basil! Sweet basil grows very well in **containers**. Plus, you can use it in many different kinds of recipes. Let's get started!

TYPES OF BASIL

LEMON BASIL

GREEK BASIL

HOLY BASIL

SWEET BASIL

THAI BASIL

LET'S GET GROWING

In this section, you'll learn how to grow basil in a **container** garden. With container gardens, you have more control over things such as light and temperature. But, keep in mind, basil grows differently in every climate.

When to Plant

Go online to find out the average date of the last frost in your area. Plant your seeds about three weeks after this date.

The Right Conditions

Sunlight
Basil is native to some of the warmest places on earth! It loves full sun for six to eight hours a day.

Temperature
*Basil seeds **germinate** at 70 to 75 **degrees**. Keep basil plants inside until temperatures are above 50 degrees at night.*

The Right Soil
Basil likes rich, warm soil that drains well.

SOW YOUR SEEDS

1   **2**   **3**

MATERIALS NEEDED

- 12-inch wide container with drainage holes
- soil
- water
- basil seeds
- spray bottle
- trowel

(1) Fill the **container** three-quarters full of soil. Wet the soil thoroughly. Sprinkle a few seeds on top. Space the seeds about 2 inches (5 cm) apart.

(2) Cover the seeds with ¼ inch (.6 cm) of soil.

Wet the soil using the spray bottle. Then place the container in a warm spot with full sun.

(3) Spray the soil often to keep it moist until the seeds **sprout**.

STAGES OF

Watering

The soil should be evenly moist, but not too wet. Water the plants in the morning. Put the water at the base of the plant, not on the leaves. Let the soil dry out a little between watering.

Thinning

Thinning means getting rid of a few basil **sprouts** so others have room to grow. When the sprouts are two inches tall, thin them. Each plant needs at least six inches of space. You can plant the ones you remove in another **container**.

WATER your basil plant in the morning. Be sure to water near the soil and not on the leaves.

THIN the sprouts when they are 2 inches (5 cm) tall.

GROWTH

Pinching

When a plant is 6 inches (15 cm) tall, pinch off the main stem directly above the third set of leaves. As the plant grows, do this for each branch. If flowers appear, pinch them off right away. You can use the leaves you pinch off in cooking.

Harvesting

Harvest the basil before autumn. After that, it will start growing flowers and stop making new leaves. The basil will also not taste very good. To harvest, cut or pinch off the stem.

PINCH off the stem above the third set of leaves. Do this every couple of weeks.

HARVEST your basil before autumn.

27

HARVESTING

BASIL

(1) Harvesting basil is as simple as pinching. Always pinch off the stem right above a set of leaves.

(2) Place the harvested stems in water. This keeps it fresh for a few days.

(3) Or you can remove the stems and put the leaves in a plastic zipper bag. Store it in the refrigerator.

(4) Before using, clean the basil in a bowl of cool water. Blot it dry.

Basil

Q&A

How long will it take to grow?

It depends on the sun, temperature, and type of basil. Most plants **mature** within 60 to 90 days.

My basil looks good, but it doesn't taste very good!

It may have been given too much **fertilizer**. This causes the plant to grow quickly, without **developing** the oils needed for flavor. Basil flavor can also be ruined by allowing flowers to grow on the plant or harvesting it too late.

Why are there black spots on the leaves?

Bacteria causes these spots. It happens when soil splashes up on the leaves. Prevent these spots by watering near the base of your plant.

Why are my leaves yellow and wilted?

The plant probably has a plant sickness called fusarium wilt. It's caused by a **fungus**. You will have to start over with new soil and new seeds.

BIG-TIME
Basil Parmesan Dip

Serve this creamy dip with oven-fresh pita chips!

MAKES 8 SERVINGS

INGREDIENTS

4 6-inch pitas

cooking spray

¼ teaspoon salt

½ teaspoon pepper

1 cup lightly packed fresh basil leaves

¾ cup Parmesan cheese, grated

¾ cup reduced-fat sour cream

2 teaspoons fresh lemon juice

1 garlic clove, pressed

TOOLS

sharp knife

cutting board

baking sheet

measuring spoons

oven mitts

measuring cups

garlic press

blender

serving bowl

1

① Preheat the oven to 375 **degrees**. Split the pitas in half. Cut each half into eight wedges.

2

② Coat the baking sheet with cooking spray. Put the pita wedges on the baking sheet. Spray them lightly with cooking spray. Sprinkle them with salt and ¼ teaspoon pepper. Bake for 12 minutes or until crisp.

3

③ Put the basil, cheese, sour cream, lemon juice, garlic, and ¼ teaspoon pepper in a blender. Blend until smooth.

4

④ Pour the dip into a serving bowl. Serve with the warm pita chips.

Even Cooler

In a hurry? Instead of making your own pita chips, buy a bag at the store.

31

PERFECT
Pizza Margherita

This classic pizza is fit for (and named after) a queen!

MAKES A 12-INCH PIZZA

INGREDIENTS

½ pound tomatoes, chopped

1 clove garlic, pressed

½ teaspoon salt

olive oil

12-inch prepared, uncooked pizza crust

6 ounces mozzarella cheese, grated

6 fresh basil leaves, julienned

¼ cup grated Parmesan cheese

TOOLS

measuring spoons

sharp knife

cutting board

garlic press

mixing bowl

mixing spoon

baking sheet

basting brush

measuring cups

oven mitts

1. Preheat the oven to 500 **degrees**. Combine the tomatoes, garlic, salt, and 2 tablespoons olive oil in a mixing bowl. Set it aside.

2. Put the pizza crust on a baking sheet. Brush it lightly with olive oil. Top the crust with the mozzarella cheese. Then add the tomato mixture. **Drizzle** olive oil over the pizza.

3. Bake for 8 to 10 minutes, until the crust is golden brown and the cheese is bubbly. Remove it from the oven. Sprinkle the Parmesan cheese and basil over the top.

4. Let the pizza cool for 2 to 3 minutes. Cut it into wedges.

Did You Know?

Italian chef Raffaele Esposito of Naples created Margherita pizza in 1889 in honor of Queen Margherita.

1

2

3

Tomato Basil Soup

This amazing soup hits the spot any day!

MAKES ABOUT 4 SERVINGS

INGREDIENTS

26 ounces canned tomatoes

2 cups tomato juice

1 cup chicken broth

¼ cup loosely packed fresh basil

1 cup whipping cream

2 tablespoons butter

Salt and pepper

TOOLS

measuring cup

blender

can opener

saucepan

mixing spoon

oven mitts

serving bowls

1. Put the tomatoes, tomato juice, and chicken broth in a saucepan. Bring it to a boil. Let it simmer for 20 minutes.

2. Carefully pour the tomato mixture into a blender. Add the basil. Blend until smooth.

3. Return the blended mixture to the saucepan. Turn the heat on low. Mix in the cream and butter until melted. Add salt and pepper to taste.

4. Put the soup in serving bowls. **Garnish** each bowl with a few basil leaves. Serve warm.

1

2

3

Thai Noodles & Basil

This easy classic is oh-so-light and delicious!

MAKES 2 TO 4 SERVINGS

INGREDIENTS

8 ounces rice noodles

1 cup fresh basil

½ cup cashews, chopped

3 garlic cloves

¼ cup olive oil

1 tablespoon fresh lime juice

1 tablespoon fish sauce

½ teaspoon cayenne pepper

2 tablespoons vegetable oil

TOOLS

large pot

oven mitts

strainer

measuring cups

measuring spoons

blender

non-stick frying pan

tongs

mixing spoon

1. Bring a large pot of water to a boil. Remove from heat and add the noodles. Let them soak about 10 minutes until they are soft but still crunchy. Strain the noodles and rinse them with cold water. Set the noodles aside.

2. Put half the basil and half the cashews in a blender. Add the garlic, olive oil, lime juice, fish sauce, and cayenne pepper. Blend until smooth.

3. Heat a large frying pan over medium-high heat. Coat it with the vegetable oil. Add the noodles. Gently turn the noodles with tongs. Stir-fry for 1 minute.

4. Put some of the basil mixture in the pan. Continue stir-frying for a couple of minutes, until the noodles are soft.

5. Remove from heat. Add the remaining basil mixture and fresh basil. Toss well. Sprinkle the remaining cashews on top.

GRILLED
Cheese & Pesto Sammy

One taste, and you'll forget regular grilled cheese!

MAKES 1 SANDWICH

INGREDIENTS

2 slices bread

1 tablespoon butter

1 tablespoon prepared pesto

1 slice provolone cheese

2 slices tomato

1 slice American cheese

TOOLS

non-stick frying pan

dinner knife

measuring spoons

spatula

sharp knife

cutting board

oven mitts

1. Heat a non-stick frying pan over medium heat. Butter one side of a bread slice. Place the slice buttered side down in the pan. Spread ½ tablespoon pesto on the bread slice.

2. Place the provolone cheese, tomato slices, and American cheese on top.

3. Spread the remaining pesto on one side of the second slice of bread. Place the slice pesto side down onto the **sandwich**. Butter the top of the sandwich.

4. When the bottom of the sandwich is golden brown, flip it over. Fry it until the second side is golden brown. Remove the sandwich from the pan. Cut it in half.

Your Own Basil Pesto!

Combine 2 cups fresh basil leaves, 1/3 cup pine nuts, 3 garlic cloves, 1/2 cup grated Parmesan, 1/2 cup olive oil, and salt and pepper to taste in a blender. Use the pulse setting until the mixture is smooth.

BEAUTEOUS
Basil-Lemon Cake

Who knew basil could be so great in a cake?

MAKES 1 CAKE

INGREDIENTS

2½ cups cake flour

2½ teaspoons baking powder

½ teaspoon salt

½ cup butter, softened

1½ cups sugar

2 large eggs, beaten

½ cup fresh basil, chopped

2 tablespoons lemon zest

1 teaspoon vanilla extract

1 cup plus 2 tablespoons buttermilk

1½ cups mixed berries

TOOLS

9-inch springform pan

measuring cups

measuring spoons

mixing bowls

oven mitts

whisk

hand mixer

zester

sharp knife

cutting board

wooden toothpicks

1 Preheat the oven to 375 **degrees**. Lightly grease the springform pan.

2 Whisk the flour, baking powder, and salt together in a medium bowl. Set it aside.

3 Put the butter and sugar in a large bowl. Beat on medium speed until creamy. Add the eggs, basil, lemon zest, and vanilla extract. Beat until smooth.

4 Add one-third of the dry mixture to the wet mixture. Beat on low speed until smooth. Add one-third of the buttermilk. Beat until smooth. Repeat, **alternating** between adding dry mixture and buttermilk.

5 Pour the batter into the springform pan. Bake for 35 to 45 minutes, or until a toothpick stuck in the center comes out clean. Let the cake cool for 10 minutes. Remove the sides of the pan. Let the cake cool completely. Cut into wedges. Serve with berries.

41

2

3

4

5

ALL ABOUT
CARROTS

Carrots are a root vegetable. They have been around for centuries! Carrots are a member of the parsley family. The parsley family also includes produce such as dill, celery, and parsnips.

There are many kinds of carrots. Carrots can be white, yellow, orange, light purple, deep red, and even black! The shape varies from short stumps to thin cones. Each looks, tastes, and grows differently.

Nantes carrots are shaped like **cylinders**. They are orange and rounded at both ends. Nantes carrots are tender and sweet. Plus, they grow well in **containers**. Let's get started!

TYPES OF CARROTS

NANTES

ATOMIC RED

DANVERS

LUNAR WHITE

SOLAR YELLOW

PURPLE
DRAGON

LET'S GET GROWING

In this section, you'll learn how to grow carrots in a **container** garden. With container gardens, you have more control over things such as light and temperature. But keep in mind that carrots grow differently in every climate.

When to Plant

Go online to find out the average date of the last frost in your area. **Sow** your carrot seeds about two weeks before this date.

The Right Conditions

Sunlight
Plants need sunlight to grow. Carrots need at least six hours of sunlight a day.

Pests and Weeds
Be earth-friendly! Soap and water sprays keep pests away. White vinegar is a great weed killer.

Temperature
*Once carrot seeds **sprout**, the ideal temperature is 60 to 70 **degrees**. If it's hotter or cooler than that, bring the container inside.*

The Right Soil
Light, sandy soils work best. Heavy, crusted-over soil can prevent carrots from sprouting. Use soil rich in organic matter. This will help your plant hold moisture.

SOW YOUR SEEDS

1 **2** **3**

MATERIALS NEEDED

10-inch deep container with drainage hole

soil

water

carrot seeds

① Fill the **container** three-quarters full of soil. Wet the soil thoroughly.

② Sprinkle the carrot seeds over the soil. You'll thin the plants later, so don't worry about how the seeds are spaced.

③ Lightly cover the seeds with ¼ inch (.6 cm) of dirt. Water lightly.

4 Carrot seeds **germinate** in soil that is 50 to 70 **degrees**. If your climate is too warm or cold, start your seeds inside.

Watering

Carrots need **consistent**, even watering. Stick your finger in the soil to check the moisture. Add water if the top 4 inches (10 cm) of the soil is dry.

Thinning

Thinning means getting rid of a few plants so others have room to grow. You will need to thin your carrots twice. Use scissors to cut away some of the **seedlings** just below the soil. Do not pull the plants out of the soil. That could **disturb** the roots of the other plants.

THIN the carrots when the tops are 2 inches (5 cm) high. There should be 1 inch (3 cm) between each carrot.

FERTILIZE when the tops are 4 inches (10 cm) high.

WATER the carrots when the top 4 inches (10 cm) of soil is dry.

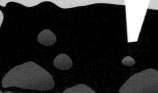

GROWTH

Fertilizing

Fertilizer has **nutrients** that help plants grow. It comes in pellets, powder, or liquid. It's often mixed with water. For carrots, use only one-half the **recommended** amount. Pour the fertilizer mix at the base of the plant, not over the leaves.

Harvesting

Harvest the carrots when they are about ½ inch (1 cm) wide. You'll see bright orange "carrot shoulders" sticking out of the ground! Harvest early for sweet, tender carrots. Leave the harvesting until later if you prefer large, heavier carrots.

FERTILIZE again when the tops are 6 inches (15 cm) high.

THIN the carrots again when you see orange roots. There should be 3 inches (8 cm) between each carrot.

HARVEST them when they are about ½ inch (1 cm) wide.

47

HARVESTING

CARROTS

① Before harvesting, **soak** the soil around the carrots with water.

② Use a garden fork or trowel to loosen the soil around the plant. Then twist the tops while pulling up.

③ Cut the tops off as soon as the carrots are out of the ground.

④ Wash the carrots and put them in plastic bags. Do not peel the carrots until you are ready to use them! Keep the carrots in the refrigerator.

Carrot Q&A

How Come My Seeds Didn't Sprout?

You should see **sprouts** within two to three weeks. Be patient! Sometimes carrot seeds can't sprout because the soil above them is too heavy, crusted, or hot.

How Long Will it Take?

Carrots take 60 to 70 days to **mature**. But growth has a lot to do with the sun and temperature.

How Do I Stop the Green Shoulders?

When the tops of carrots are above the soil line, they turn green. Covering the carrot "shoulders" with soil stops this problem.

Why Are My Carrots Twisted Around Each Other?

Carrots twist when they are too crowded. That's why thinning is important. Twisted carrots are still tasty. They just look funny!

What's With the Split or Hairy Carrots?

Not watering properly can make carrots split or grow hairy roots. Water carrots **consistently** and evenly.

CHILLY
Dilly Carrot Dip

The best thing to happen to carrots since thinning!

MAKES 4 SERVINGS

INGREDIENTS

1 garlic clove
4 sprigs of fresh dill
½ teaspoon salt
¼ teaspoon pepper
12 ounces sour cream
¼ cup mayonnaise
carrots for dipping

TOOLS

garlic press
cutting board
sharp knife
measuring spoons
measuring cups
mixing bowl
mixing spoon
serving bowl
peeler

1. Press the garlic and chop the dill.

2. Put the garlic, dill, salt, pepper, sour cream, and mayonnaise in a mixing bowl. Mix well.

3. Put the dip in a smaller serving bowl. Put it in the refrigerator for at least one hour.

4. Peel the carrots. Cut off the ends. Cut the carrots in quarters lengthwise.

5. **Garnish** the dip with some fresh dill. Serve it with the fresh carrot sticks.

Even Cooler

This dip is great with any kind of veggie! Try celery, cucumbers, or tomatoes. It's great with chips or pita bread too!

51

1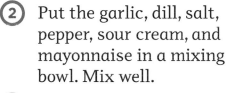

2

3

5

PICKLED
Carrot Sticks

Cucumbers aren't the only veggies that taste great pickled!

MAKES 1 PINT

INGREDIENTS

4 to 6 carrots, peeled

1 cup cider vinegar

¼ cup sugar

2 garlic cloves, pressed

1½ teaspoons fennel seeds

1½ tablespoons coarse salt

2 bay leaves

TOOLS

medium-sized pot

cutting board

sharp knife

strainer

pint jar with cover

measuring cups

measuring spoons

ladle or canning funnel

peeler

grater

① Bring a medium-sized pot of water to a boil. In the meantime, make the carrot sticks. Remove the ends of the carrots. Cut the carrots lengthwise. Then cut the carrots crosswise into thirds. This leaves six pieces per carrot. Cut the bigger pieces lengthwise again. They should all be about the same width.

② Put the carrots in the boiling water. Simmer for one minute. Pour them into a strainer and rinse under cold water. Strain thoroughly. When the carrots are cool, put them in the jar.

③ In the same pot, heat the vinegar, sugar, garlic, fennel seeds, salt, bay leaves, and 1¼ cup water. When it begins to boil, reduce the heat and simmer for two minutes.

④ Remove the pot from the heat. Cool until room temperature. This is the brine. Use a ladle or a canning funnel to put the brine in the jar. Cover the jar and chill in the refrigerator for at least one day.

1

2

3

4

CREAMY
Carrot Soup

This amazing soup is so creamy it's dreamy!

MAKES 6 SERVINGS

INGREDIENTS

8 large carrots, peeled and sliced

1½ cups chicken broth

2 garlic cloves, pressed

zest from 1 whole lemon

1½ cups half-and-half

2 tablespoon lemon juice

¼ teaspoon nutmeg

salt and pepper to taste

fresh basil

TOOLS

peeler

cutting board

sharp knife

measuring cups

garlic press

zester

large pot

mixing spoon

blender

measuring spoons

ladle

serving bowls

1. Put the carrots, chicken broth, garlic, and lemon zest in a large pot. Bring to a boil. Reduce heat and simmer for 20 minutes. Remove from heat.

2. Carefully pour the mixture into the blender. Have an adult help you. Blend until smooth.

3. Pour the mixture back into the large pot. Add the half-and-half, lemon juice, and nutmeg. Stir well. Add salt and pepper to taste. Over low heat, warm the soup to serving temperature.

4. Put the soup in serving bowls. **Garnish** with fresh basil.

Carrot Bake

This warm, cheesy side dish goes with any meal!

MAKES 4 SERVINGS

INGREDIENTS

8 medium carrots, peeled and sliced

¾ cup mayonnaise

2 tablespoons onion, finely chopped

1 tablespoon horseradish

1 teaspoon salt

¼ teaspoon pepper

2 tablespoons butter, softened

½ cup bread crumbs

½ cup colby cheese, grated

TOOLS

peeler

cutting board

sharp knife

grater

8 × 8-inch baking dish

medium-sized pot

strainer

measuring cups

measuring spoons

mixing bowls

mixing spoon

1. Preheat the oven to 350 **degrees**. Grease the bottom and sides of the baking dish.

2. Bring a medium-sized pot of water to a boil. Add the sliced carrots. Reduce the heat. Simmer for 2 minutes. Strain the carrots and place them in the bottom of the baking dish.

3. Put the mayonnaise, onion, horseradish, salt, pepper, and ⅓ cup water in a small bowl. Mix well. Pour the mixture over the carrots.

4. Mix the softened butter and bread crumbs together. Sprinkle it over the top of the carrots. Bake for 25 to 30 minutes. The top should be lightly **toasted**.

5. Remove the dish from the oven. Sprinkle the grated cheese on top. Return it to the oven for 2 to 3 minutes or until cheese is melted.

Carrot Muffins

These tasty muffins are just as good as carrot cake!

MAKES 12 MUFFINS

INGREDIENTS

⅔ cup raisins

1⅓ cups all-purpose flour

2 teaspoons baking powder

1¼ teaspoons baking soda

¾ teaspoon salt

¾ teaspoon ground cinnamon

2¾ eggs

⅔ cup vegetable oil

½ cup brown sugar

2 cups carrots, grated

TOOLS

measuring cups

mixing bowls

strainer

12-muffin tin

12 paper liners

measuring spoons

whisk

mixing spoon

grater

serving spoon

1. Put the raisins and 1⅓ cup warm water in a small bowl. Let **soak** for 15 minutes. Strain the raisins. Set them aside.

2. Preheat the oven to 350 **degrees**. Line the muffin tin with paper muffin liners.

3. Put the flour, baking powder, baking soda, salt, and cinnamon in a large bowl. Whisk together well. Set aside.

4. In a separate bowl, combine eggs, oil, and brown sugar. Whisk well. Add the egg mixture to the flour mixture. Mix just until moistened. Fold in carrots and raisins.

5. Use a serving spoon to put the carrot mixture in the muffin tin. Bake for 25 minutes. The muffins should rise and be golden brown on top. Let them cool for 30 minutes.

1

3

4

5

Green beans have a lot of names. They are called French beans, string beans, or snap beans. Some green beans are actually yellow. Others are purple!

Green bean pods are harvested before the seeds inside begin to **bulge**. Then we eat them, pod and all!

There are two main groups of green beans. "Pole beans" grow up poles or **trellises**. They can grow more than ten feet tall! "Bush bean" plants are short. They only get about two feet tall, so they don't need a pole or trellis for support.

TYPES OF BEANS

PURPLE QUEEN

SCARLET RUNNER

GOLD
MINE

KENTUCKY
BLUE

LET'S GET
GROWING

In this section, you'll learn how to grow green beans in a **container** garden. With container gardens, you have more control over things such as light and temperature. But keep in mind that green beans grow differently in every climate.

When to Plant

Go online to find the average date of the last frost in your area. Plant your seeds about three weeks after this date. Beans don't like the cold!

The Right Conditions

Sunlight
Green beans need full sun. They should be in the sun for six to eight hours a day.

Temperature
*Bean seeds **germinate** when the temperature is between 70 and 80 **degrees**. Bean plants do best in temperatures between 75 and 90 degrees.*

The Right Soil
Green beans need soil that is fertile and drains easily.

SOW YOUR SEEDS

MATERIALS NEEDED

1-gallon container with drainage holes

potting soil mix

green bean seeds

water

spray bottle

1. Fill the **container** with soil. Use your finger to make three holes in the soil. Space the holes out evenly. They should be at least 1 inch (3 cm) from the side of the container. Each hole should be about 1 inch (3 cm) deep.

2. Put two to three green bean seeds in each hole. Cover lightly with soil.

3. Use the spray bottle to moisten the soil well. Place the container in a warm spot with full sun. Keep the soil moist until the seeds **sprout**.

STAGES OF

Watering

The soil should be evenly moist, but not **waterlogged**. Always water your plants in the morning. Direct the water toward the base of the plant. Try not to get the leaves wet.

Mulching

Mulch helps keep your green bean plants warm. They love heat! Mulch also keeps moisture in. Place mulch around your plants when they are about 2 inches (5 cm) tall.

WATER your bean plant in the morning. Be sure to water near the soil and not above the leaves.

MULCH your green bean plants when they are 2 inches (5 cm) tall.

GROWTH

Fertilizing

Fertilizer has **nutrients** that help plants grow. It comes in pellets, powder, or liquid. Green beans will respond well to water **soluble** fertilizers. Use fertilizer once a month.

Harvesting

Harvest your green beans before the pods bulge. The pods should "snap" when you break them in half. After all, that's how they got the name "snap beans"!

FERTILIZE the soil around your plant once every month. Use water soluble fertilizer.

HARVEST your green bean pods when they are crisp and can be easily snapped in half.

HARVESTING

GREEN BEANS

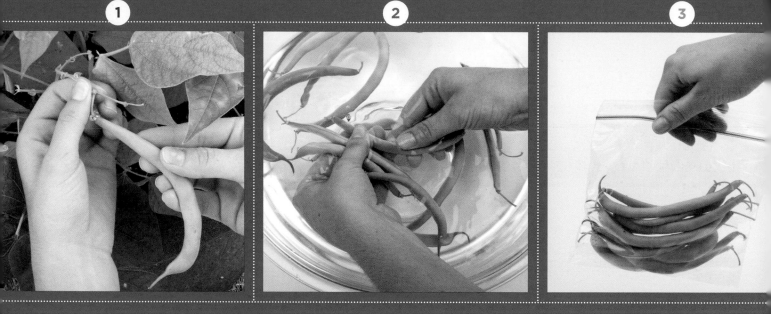

① Handle your bean plants carefully. Use one hand to hold the stem, and one hand to remove the pod. Always harvest pods when the plant is dry.

② Wash the beans in a bowl of cold water. Then put them in a strainer and rinse them with cold water.

③ Store your green beans in a sealed plastic bag. They will last longer if you keep them in the refrigerator.

Green Bean
Q & A

How long will it take to grow?

It depends on the sun, temperature, and type of green beans. Most green bean plants will produce pods in about 60 days.

Why is my green bean plant not producing many pods?

It could be too hot. If it is very hot and dry, the flowers might fall off before they can form pods.

Why are there spots on my leaves?

This is most likely a **fungus** problem caused by moisture. Remove the affected parts of the plant right away. When you water, make sure you direct the water at the soil and not the leaves.

DID YOU KNOW?

- Yellow and purple beans taste the same as green beans.

- Purple beans turn green when they are cooked.

- Eating more green beans can make your heart stronger and healthier!

SPICY
Sesame Green Beans

This dish will turn bean haters into bean lovers!

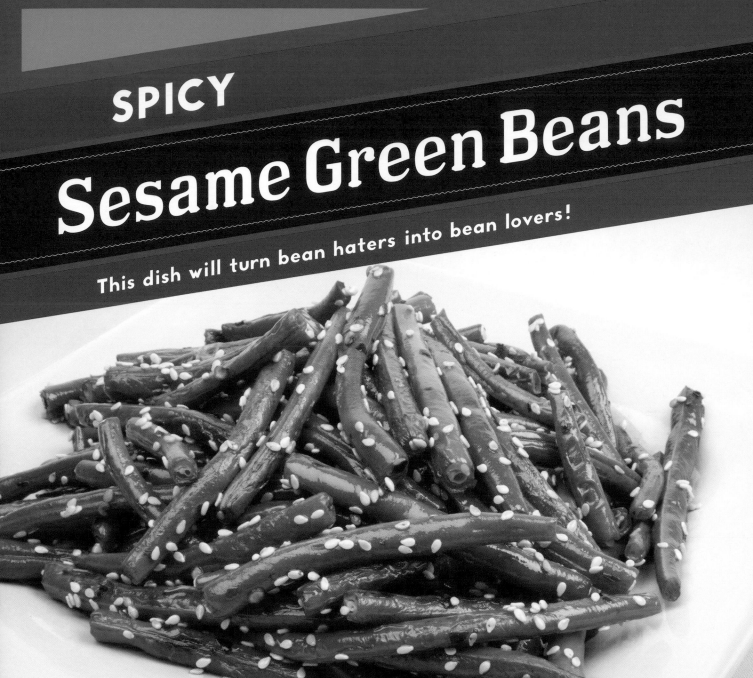

MAKES 4 SERVINGS

INGREDIENTS

2 tablespoons
sesame seeds

4½ cups raw green
beans, ends trimmed

1 tablespoon
vegetable oil

1 teaspoon sesame oil

½ teaspoon red pepper
flakes, crushed

salt

TOOLS

measuring spoons

frying pan

small bowl

saucepan

measuring cups

strainer

mixing spoon

sharp knife

cutting board

pot holders

① Put the sesame seeds in a frying pan. Toast them over medium heat, shaking the pan frequently. When the seeds start to smell strongly, they are done! Put the seeds in a small bowl.

② Put ½ inch (1 cm) of water in a saucepan. Bring it to a boil. Add the beans and simmer for 2 minutes. Pour the beans into a strainer and rinse under cold water. Drain well.

3 Heat the frying pan over high heat. Add the vegetable oil and swirl it to cover the bottom of the pan. Add the sesame oil and crushed pepper flakes. Be careful. The pan will smoke!

④ Quickly add the beans and stir-fry for 2 minutes. Add the sesame seeds and a **pinch** of salt. Toss to coat beans evenly.

69

1

2

4

Green Bean Penne

Enjoy the crunchy beans and creamy cheese contrast!

MAKES 5 TO 6 SERVINGS

INGREDIENTS

4½ cups raw
green beans

salt

16 ounces penne pasta

⅓ lb. blue cheese

½ cup mayonnaise

2 tablespoons
red wine vinegar

3 tablespoons
parsley, chopped

3 tablespoons
chives, chopped

½ cup almonds, chopped

½ teaspoon pepper

TOOLS

measuring cups

2 large pots

pot holders

measuring spoons

sharp knife

cutting board

strainer

blender

mixing bowls

mixing spoon

① Remove the stems from the beans. Bring two large pots of salted water to a boil. Add the beans to one pot of boiling water and the pasta to the other.

2 Boil the green beans 1 minute. Quickly drain and rinse them in cold water. Cut the beans into 1-inch (3 cm) pieces and set them aside. Cook the pasta as long as the directions on the package say to. Drain and rinse the pasta under cold water until cool.

③ Put the blue cheese, mayonnaise, and vinegar in a blender. Blend until mixed but still slightly lumpy.

④ In a large mixing bowl, toss together the pasta, green beans, blue cheese mixture, parsley, chives, almonds, and pepper. Add salt to taste.

71

Green Bean Salad

This fresh and tasty salad uses beans and bean sprouts!

MAKES ABOUT 4 SERVINGS

INGREDIENTS

4½ cups raw green beans, ends trimmed

salt

¼ cup olive oil

2 medium shallots, finely chopped

2 tablespoons tarragon, chopped

pepper

1 pint cherry tomatoes, halved

1 cup fresh bean sprouts

TOOLS

measuring cups

sharp knife

cutting board

large pot

pot holders

strainer

measuring spoons

mixing bowls

whisk

mixing spoons

1. Bring a large pot of salted water to a boil. Add the beans and cook them for 4 minutes, or until just tender. Drain the beans and rinse them under cold water until cool. Set the beans aside.

2. Put the olive oil, shallots, and tarragon in a small mixing bowl. Add salt and pepper to taste. Whisk them together.

3. Put the beans, tomatoes, and bean **sprouts** in a large mixing bowl. Add the olive oil mixture and toss well.

1

2

3

73

BREATHTAKING
Bean & Ham Soup

This authentic classic will amaze your guests!

MAKES 6 TO 8 SERVINGS

INGREDIENTS

1 meaty ham bone

4 cups green beans, cut to 1-inch pieces

4 potatoes, cubed

1 onion, chopped

¾ cup parsley, chopped

1 tablespoon fresh thyme

3 tablespoons butter

3 tablespoons all-purpose flour

1 cup half-and-half

salt and pepper to taste

TOOLS

measuring cups

large pot with cover

pot holders

fork

sharp knife

cutting board

measuring spoons

frying pan

whisk

spatula

1 Put the ham bone and 8 cups of water in a large pot. Cover and bring it to a boil. Cook for 1½ to 2 hours. Remove the ham and set it aside. The water in the pot is called the soup stock. Keep it warm on low heat.

2 Ask an adult to help you cut the meat off the bone using a fork and sharp knife. Chop the meat and put it back in the stock.

3 Add the beans, potatoes, onions, parsley, and thyme. Simmer for about 10 minutes, or until the potatoes are tender.

4 Melt the butter in a small frying pan. While whisking constantly, slowly add the flour. Whisk until the mixture is golden. Be careful. It burns easily! This butter and flour mixture is called the roux.

5 When the potatoes are tender, add the roux and the half-and-half. Stir until well mixed. The soup will thicken.

CHEDDAR PECAN

Green Bean Casserole

Green bean casserole just got a major upgrade!

MAKES 6 TO 8 SERVINGS

INGREDIENTS

2 tablespoons butter

¼ cup all-purpose flour

1½ cups milk

½ cup buttermilk

1 tablespoon ranch dressing mix

¼ teaspoon salt

¼ teaspoon pepper

4½ cups raw green beans, ends trimmed

non-stick cooking spray

1 cup cheddar cheese, grated

½ cup Panko

½ cup pecans, chopped

TOOLS

2 large pots

pot holders

measuring cups & spoons

whisk

sharp knife

cutting board

strainer

spatula

9 x 9-inch baking dish

mixing bowl

1. Preheat oven to 350 **degrees**. Melt the butter in a large pot over medium heat. Whisk in the flour. Cook 1 minute, whisking constantly. Add the milk. Still whisking constantly, cook for 3 to 4 minutes until mixture is thick. This is the white sauce.

2. Remove the pot from the heat. Whisk in the buttermilk, ranch dressing mix, salt, and pepper. Set the sauce aside.

3. In another large pot, boil the green beans in salted water for 4 minutes. Drain and rinse with cool water.

4. Spray the baking dish lightly with cooking spray. Toss the white sauce, ½ cup cheese, and the green beans together in a large bowl. Pour it into the baking dish.

5. Sprinkle the Panko, pecans, and remaining cheese over the green bean mixture. Bake for 25 to 30 minutes, or until golden brown.

77

Citrus Zest Beans

This startling bean dish is almost a dessert!

MAKES 4 SERVINGS

INGREDIENTS

2½ cups raw green beans, ends trimmed

2 tablespoons olive oil

salt and pepper

¼ teaspoon lemon zest

¼ teaspoon lime zest

2 tablespoons chives, chopped

1 tablespoon fresh lemon juice

TOOLS

sharp knife

cutting board

measuring cups

measuring spoons

zester

frying pan with lid

mixing spoon

① Choose beans that are about ¼ inch (.6 cm) thick. Carefully slice each bean into pieces at an angle.

② Heat the oil in a medium frying pan. Add the beans and cook over high heat for 1 minute, stirring constantly. Add 2 tablespoons water. Add salt and pepper to taste. Cover and cook the beans for 2 minutes.

③ Add the lemon and lime zest and the chives. Stirring constantly, cook for 2 to 3 minutes, or until beans are tender.

4 Stir in the lemon juice. Serve warm.

Did You Know?
If you don't have a zester, you can use the smallest holes on a grater!

LEAF LETTUCE

Lettuce has been around for centuries. We know that Egyptians have been eating it for more than 4,500 years! Today there are many **varieties** of lettuce. They all look, taste, and grow differently.

Leaf lettuce is one group of lettuce. It has loose leaves with curly edges. Its color can range from light green to red. Leaf lettuce tastes light and mild. But each variety tastes a little different from the others!

TYPES OF LETTUCE

ROYAL OAK LEAF

SALAD BOWL

BRAVEHEART

GREEN
ICE

BUTTERCRUNCH

LET'S GET
GROWING

In this section, you'll learn how to grow leaf lettuce in **containers**. Leaf lettuce is one of the easiest types of lettuce to grow. Plus, it grows fast. Let's get started!

When to Plant

Go online to find out the average date of the last frost in your area. **Sow** your lettuce seeds after this date.

The Right Conditions

Sunlight
Plants need sunlight to grow. Leave your lettuce plants in the sun for three to six hours a day.

Pests and Weeds
Be earth-friendly! Soap and water sprays keep pests away. White vinegar is a great weed killer.

Temperature
*Once lettuce seeds **sprout**, the ideal temperature is 50 to 70 **degrees**. If it's hotter or cooler than that, bring the container inside.*

Shade
Plant in an area with some natural shade. Or use shade cloth to keep your plants cool when it is really hot out.

The Right Soil
*Leaf lettuce needs a lot of **nutrients** in its soil! Choose a loose **loam** that is rich in organic matter, **nitrogen**, and **fertilizers**.*

SOW YOUR SEEDS

MATERIALS NEEDED

6-inch deep container with drainage hole

soil

water

leaf lettuce seeds

1. Fill the **container** three-quarters full of soil. Wet the soil thoroughly.

2. Sprinkle the seeds over the the soil. You'll thin the plants later, so don't worry about how the seeds are spaced.

3. Lightly cover the seeds with ⅛ inch (.3 cm) of dirt. Water lightly.

4. Leaf lettuce seeds **germinate** in soil that is 45 to 70 **degrees**. If your climate is too warm or cold, start your seeds inside.

Watering

Leaf lettuce loves water. Keep the soil moist, but not **waterlogged**. Before the **seedlings sprout**, use a spray bottle. After sprouts appear, use a watering can. Don't let the plants dry out!

Fertilizing

Lettuce likes to eat too! The more it eats, the faster it grows. The faster it grows, the better it tastes! For best results, add **fish emulsion** to your plants every week.

Thinning

Thinning means removing a few plants so others have room to grow. Leave 3 to 4 inches (8 to 10 cm) between plants. You can plant the ones you remove in another **container**.

WATER your lettuce plants whenever the soil is dry.

THIN the plants when the lettuce is about 2 inches (5 cm) tall.

FERTILIZE with fish emulsion every week.

MULCH right after thinning the lettuce.

GROWTH

Mulching

If you live in a dry climate, use **mulch** to keep the plants moist. After thinning the plants, spread a 2-inch (5 cm) layer of organic mulch around each one.

Trimming

Use a scissors to cut off the outside leaves. Try them in a salad! Removing the outside leaves helps the inside leaves grow.

Harvesting

You don't have to harvest leaf lettuce. You can just keep trimming it! But if you want to harvest it, use a scissors to cut the plants about 1 inch (3 cm) above the soil. That way they will grow back!

TRIM the lettuce when it gets about 3 inches (8 cm) tall.

HARVEST when the lettuce is 4 to 5 inches (10 to 13 cm) high.

85

HARVESTING

LEAF LETTUCE

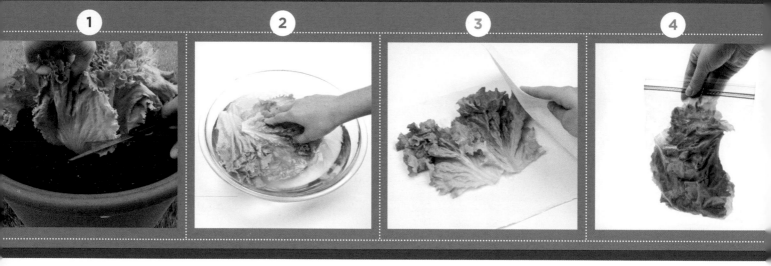

(1) Cut the plant with a scissors. Leave about 1 inch (3 cm) above the soil. It will grow back in a few weeks!

(2) Separate the leaves. Fill the sink or a large **container** with cool water. Put the leaves in and swish them around. Then put them in a strainer and give the leaves one more rinse.

(3) Spread some paper towels on the counter. Lay the lettuce on top and blot it dry with more paper towels. Use linen towels if you can.

(4) Store the clean, dry lettuce in a plastic zipper bag. Push the air out before zipping it. Store it in the refrigerator. Lettuce will usually keep for six to eight days.

Leaf Lettuce

Q & A

How Come My Seeds Didn't Sprout?

You should see **sprouts** within one to two weeks. Be patient! Sometimes the seeds are planted too deep. Sometimes they get too much water. Just try again.

How Long Will it Take?

Leaf lettuce takes 40 to 60 days to **mature.** But growth has a lot to do with the sun and temperature. Leaf lettuce will grow the fastest in the summer.

Why Did My Plants Bolt on Me?

Leaf lettuce bolts, or turns to seed, near the end of its life. Bolting cannot be stopped once it's started. Leaf lettuce only lasts one season. You can look forward to planting more seeds next year!

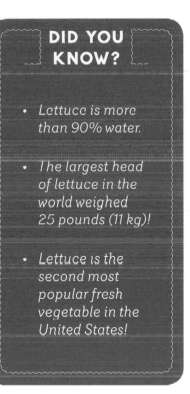

DID YOU KNOW?

- Lettuce is more than 90% water.

- The largest head of lettuce in the world weighed 25 pounds (11 kg)!

- Lettuce is the second most popular fresh vegetable in the United States!

SORT-OF
Sushi Rolls

Roll your own sushi with lettuce!

INGREDIENTS

½ cup uncooked, long-grain rice

¼ cup rice vinegar

1 large, ripe avocado

1 carrot, peeled

1 cucumber, peeled

4 pieces of leaf lettuce, cleaned and dried

soy sauce

TOOLS

measuring cups

mixing bowls

mixing spoon

fork

peeler

cutting board

sharp knife

measuring spoons

1

2

3

5

① Prepare the rice according to the package instructions. Place the cooked rice in a medium-sized bowl, and spread it out. Pour the vinegar evenly over the rice. Pour it a little at a time. The rice should be slightly moistened. Gently stir with a large spoon. Let the rice mixture cool. Then fluff it with a fork.

② Peel the avocado. Remove the seed. Mash it until smooth.

③ Use the peeler to slice off thin strips of carrot. Cut the ends off of the cucumber. Slice it into ¼-inch (.5 cm) strips.

4 Spread about 1 tablespoon of mashed avocado onto a lettuce leaf. Add a few tablespoons of rice. Flatten out the rice. Place some cucumber and carrot on top.

⑤ Roll the lettuce leaf. Serve with soy sauce and rice.

ROCK-ON
Raisin Salad

Guaranteed to please all raisin lovers!

MAKES 2 SALADS

INGREDIENTS

2 tablespoons
mayonnaise

2 teaspoons Dijon
mustard

2 teaspoons honey

1 teaspoon lemon
juice

pinch of salt

leaf lettuce, cleaned
and dried

¼ cup raisins

¼ cup golden raisins

croutons

TOOLS

measuring spoons

jar with a lid

2 serving bowls

measuring cups

serving spoon

① Make the dressing for the salad first. Put the mayonnaise, mustard, honey, lemon juice, and salt in the jar. Close the lid. Shake well.

② Tear the lettuce into bite-size pieces. Put some in each serving bowl.

③ Put half of the raisins and golden raisins in each bowl. Use a serving spoon to drizzle dressing over the salads. Add croutons to taste.

To Taste?

Sometimes a recipe says to add an ingredient "to taste." That means you decide how much to add! Start small. You can always add more later. It's harder to remove something than it is to add more!

91

1

2

3

BRIGHT BEGINNING
Breakfast Wrap

Chances are, you'll want these for lunch and dinner too!

MAKES 4 WRAPS

INGREDIENTS

2 tablespoons refried beans

2 tablespoons salsa

3 eggs, beaten

1 tablespoon mayonnaise

4 flour tortillas

1½ cups lettuce, shredded (see page 17)

TOOLS

measuring spoons

mixing bowls

mixing spoon

non-stick frying pan

whisk

spatula

measuring cups

dinner knife

1. Put the beans and salsa in a small bowl. Mix until smooth. Heat the frying pan over medium heat.

2. Whisk the eggs in a small bowl. Pour the eggs into the frying pan. Wait about 1 minute. The bottom of the eggs should be slightly hard.

3. Pour the bean mixture over one half of the eggs. Use a spatula to flip the other half on top of the beans. Cook a couple more minutes until the eggs are set.

4. Spread some of the mayonnaise on each tortilla. Cut the eggs into four equal pieces. Put one piece on each tortilla. Cover the eggs with shredded lettuce. Roll up the tortillas.

1

2

3

4

BERRY GOOD
Vinaigrette Salad

Fresh berries make this tangy salad a sensation!

INGREDIENTS

2 tablespoons pecans, chopped

1 tablespoon vinegar

3 tablespoons olive oil

1 teaspoon lemon juice

salt and pepper

leaf lettuce, cleaned and dried

⅔ cup fresh strawberries, diced

2 tablespoons crumbled blue cheese

TOOLS

measuring spoons

cutting board

sharp knife

non-stick frying pan

mixing spoon

mixing bowls

whisk

① Put the pecans in the frying pan over medium heat. Stir them frequently until lightly toasted. Remove from heat.

② Make the dressing. Put the vinegar, olive oil, lemon juice, salt and pepper in a bowl. Whisk thoroughly.

③ Tear the lettuce into bite-size pieces. Put it in a large bowl. Add the toasted pecans, strawberries, and blue cheese. Toss with the dressing before serving.

1

2

3

95

THE AMAZING
ALT Sandwich

A tasty, tempting alternative to the BLT!

MAKES 2 SANDWICHES

INGREDIENTS

1 avocado

4 slices whole-grain bread

2 tablespoons mayonnaise

8 large pieces of leaf lettuce, cleaned and dried

1 tomato, thinly sliced

TOOLS

cutting board

sharp knife

spoon

toaster

dinner knife

1. Cut all the way around the avocado lengthwise. Do not try to cut through the pit. Then twist and pull to separate into two halves.

2. Carefully remove the pit. Cut each half lengthwise. Do not cut through the skin. Use a spoon to gently scoop out the avocado.

3. Cut the scooped avocado into thin slices.

4. Toast the bread. Spread some mayonnaise on each slice.

5. Put two lettuce leaves on each slice of toast. Put tomato on two of the slices. Put avocado on the other two slices.

6. Turn the slices with tomato over on top of the slices with avocado. Cut each sandwich in half.

NACHO AVERAGE

Taco Bowl

Why dirty a dish when you can make your own?

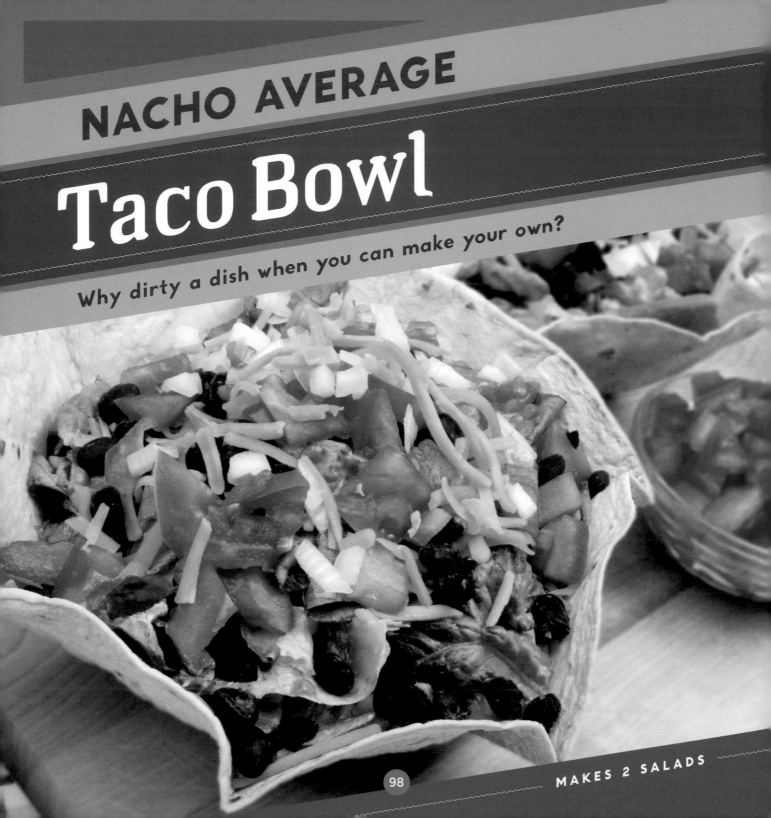

MAKES 2 SALADS

INGREDIENTS

1 tablespoon lime juice

3 tablespoons sour cream

1½ tablespoons olive oil

1 teaspoon cumin

2 flour tortillas

olive oil

1 can black beans, rinsed

4 cups leaf lettuce, shredded (see page 17)

salt and pepper

1 cup cheddar cheese, shredded

1 small tomato, chopped

1 can black olives, drained

½ onion, finely chopped

TOOLS

measuring cups & spoons

mixing bowls

whisk

can opener

2 oven-safe glass bowls

baking sheet

strainer

sharp knife

cutting board

mixing spoon

1

2

4

5

① Preheat the oven to 400 **degrees**. Make the dressing. Put the lime juice, sour cream, olive oil, and cumin in a bowl. Whisk thoroughly.

② Microwave the tortillas for 10 seconds. Rub a thin coat of olive oil over each tortilla. Place two oven-safe glass bowls upside down on a baking sheet. Put a tortilla over each bowl. The tortillas should not touch the baking sheet. Gently press the tortillas around the bowls. Bake for 8 to 10 minutes.

3 Remove the tortillas from the oven. While they cool, warm up the black beans in the microwave. Put them in a bowl first.

④ Put the lettuce, salt and pepper, and salad dressing in a large bowl. Toss well. Put half the lettuce mixture in each tortilla bowl.

⑤ Put shredded cheese on each salad. Then add some warm black beans. Add the tomato, black olives, and onion last.

99

ALL ABOUT
POTATOES

Potatoes are one of the world's main food crops. It's easy to see why! You can grow a lot of potatoes with less work than many other foods. They also adapt well to different climates. They grow and can be stored underground!

There are more than 5,000 kinds of potatoes. Each looks, tastes, and grows differently! In this book, we're going to grow and cook Yukon Golds. Yukon Golds are a kind of yellow potato, and they grow very well in **containers**. Let's get started!

TYPES OF POTATOES

RUSSIAN BANANA

ROSE FIN APPLE

YUKON GOLD

DAISY GOLD

LET'S GET
GROWING

In this section, you'll learn how to grow potatoes in a **container** garden. With container gardens, you have more control over things such as light and temperature. But keep in mind that potatoes grow differently in every climate.

When to Plant

Go online to find out the average date of the last frost in your area. Plant your seed potatoes about two weeks before this date.

The Right Conditions

Sunlight
Potato plants need six to eight hours of sunlight a day.

Temperature
*Potato plants will not grow until the soil temperature has reached 45 **degrees**. They grow best between 60 and 70 degrees.*

The Right Soil
Potatoes take a lot of nutrients from the soil. They need fertile, loose, well-draining loam.

SOW YOUR

SEEDS

MATERIALS NEEDED

5-gallon container with drainage holes

potting soil mix

2-inch-wide, certified-organic seed potato, sprouted

water

trowel

(1) Fill the **container** one-third full of soil. Put the seed potato on top. Add just enough soil to cover it. Water it immediately.

(2) When the plant is about 6 inches (15 cm) tall, add a hill of soil around the plant. The hill should be 2 to 3 inches (5 to 7 cm) high.

(3) Every time the plant grows 6 inches (15 cm) taller than the soil, add another hill. This is called *hilling*.

4 Continue hilling until the soil is about 1 to 2 inches (2.5 to 5 cm) from the top of the container.

STAGES OF

Watering

The soil should be evenly moist, but not too wet. Always water your plants in the morning. Stop watering the potato plant when the leaves turn yellow.

Hilling

Hilling is when you add more soil around the plant. The new potatoes grow above the original seed potato. That's why hilling is important. Use **compost** whenever you can.

WATER the plant in the morning. Keep the soil evenly moist.

HILL the plant when it is 6 inches (15 cm) tall.

HILL the plant again each time there are 6 inches (15 cm) showing above the soil.

FERTILIZE once a month. Add water soluble fertilizer when you water the plant.

GROWTH

Fertilizing

Find a high-quality **fertilizer** that is water **soluble**. Use it once a month when you water your plant. Your potato plant will love you.

Harvesting

Most potato plants live for about four months above ground. Then they begin to wilt. When the leaves turn brown and die, the potatoes are **mature** and ready to eat!

Don't WATER after the leaves turn yellow.

HARVEST the potatoes when the plant grows flowers and the leaves turn brown.

HARVESTING

POTATOES

(1) Before harvesting, get the soil around the potatoes very wet.

(2) Use a shovel or garden fork to help dig the potatoes out of the soil. Be careful not to **damage** them!

(3) Before using the potatoes, **scrub** them with a vegetable brush. Rinse them in cold water.

4 Store potatoes in a dark, cool place. The ideal storage temperature is about 40 **degrees**.

Potato Q&A

QUESTIONS & ANSWERS

How long will it take?

It depends on the sun, temperature and type of potato. Most potatoes are ready in 70 to 90 days.

Why are there black spots in the middle of my potatoes?

Black or hollow centers are caused by over-watering. When you water, the soil should be thoroughly wet. But don't let it become **waterlogged**.

Why are my potatoes shaped funny?

Not watering often enough can cause the potatoes to have bumps.

Why are there black spots on the leaves of my potato plant?

Potato **blight** attacks the leaves first. Then the potatoes. If your leaves have black spots, cut down the plant. Leave just 2 inches (5 cm) of stem above the soil. This results in a smaller harvest, but at least you'll get a few potatoes!

OH, YEAH!
Oven Fries

A simple and tasty way to enjoy potatoes!

MAKES 6 SERVINGS

INGREDIENTS

non-stick cooking
spray

2½ pounds
yellow potatoes

1 teaspoon
vegetable oil

1 tablespoon sugar

1 teaspoon salt

cayenne pepper

TOOLS

baking sheet

aluminum foil

cutting board

sharp knife

mixing bowl

measuring spoons

pasta server

oven mitts

1   Preheat the oven to 450 **degrees**.
    Line a baking sheet with aluminum
    foil. Coat the foil with non-stick
    cooking spray.

2   Wash and **scrub** the potatoes. Cut
    each potato in half lengthwise.

3   Place a potato half flat-side down on
    the cutting board. Cut it lengthwise
    into ½-inch (1 cm) strips.

4   Remove the two end strips. Turn the
    sliced potato half on its side. Stack
    the strips evenly. Cut the stack
    lengthwise into ½-inch (1 cm) strips.

5   Repeat steps 3 and 4 for each
    potato half.

6   Put the potato strips in a large
    bowl. Add the oil, sugar, salt, and
    a **pinch** of cayenne pepper. Toss to
    coat the potatoes.

7   Put the potatoes on the baking
    sheet in an even layer. Bake for
    30 minutes, or until potatoes are
    tender and browned.

3

4

6

7

Potato Soup

This creamy soup is sure to please!

MAKES 6 TO 8 SERVINGS

INGREDIENTS

6 yellow potatoes, peeled

1 onion

½ cup butter, cut into chunks

½ cup flour

1 cup cooked ham, diced

1 teaspoon parsley flakes

2 cups milk

salt and pepper

TOOLS

large pot

cutting board

sharp knife

strainer

large bowl

pot holders

mixing spoon

measuring cups

measuring spoons

---

1. Boil a large pot of water. While it is heating up, chop the potatoes and onion. Add both to the boiling water. Cook for about 10 minutes, or until potatoes are tender.

2. Hold or set a strainer over a large bowl. Ask an adult to help carefully empty the pot into the strainer. Measure 4 cups of the potato water. Set it aside.

3. Put the potatoes and onions back in the pot. Turn the heat to low. Add the butter. Stir until the butter is melted

4. Add the flour, ham, and parsley. Stir lightly. Add the milk and potato water. Turn the heat up to medium. Stir until the soup thickens. This takes about 5 minutes. Add salt and pepper to taste.

5. Put the soup in serving bowls. **Garnish** each bowl with a few leaves of parsley.

TEMPTING
Twice-Baked Potatoes

These tasty spuds can be an appetizer or main dish!

MAKES 4 SERVINGS

INGREDIENTS

2 yellow potatoes

¼ cup cheddar cheese,
grated

2 tablespoons butter

2 tablespoons milk

2 tablespoons onion,
chopped

salt and pepper

1 tablespoon
green onions, chopped

TOOLS

fork

oven mitts

spoon

mixing bowl

grater

measuring cups

measuring spoons

cutting board

sharp knife

baking sheet

① Preheat the oven to 400 **degrees**. Poke each potato several times with a fork. Bake the potatoes in the preheated oven for 45 minutes. To see if they are done, stick a fork in one. The fork should enter easily.

② Once the potatoes are done, remove them from the oven. Let the potatoes cool slightly. Cut each potato in half lengthwise. Scoop out the insides with a spoon. Put the potato insides in a bowl. Set the empty skins aside.

③ Put the cheese, butter, milk, and onion in the bowl with the potato. Add salt and pepper to taste. Mix with a fork until smooth. Put one-fourth of the potato mixture in each of the potato skins.

④ Set the potatoes on a baking sheet. Bake for 10 minutes, or until the tops are golden brown. Sprinkle the chopped green onions over the potatoes.

1

2

3

4

FANTASTIC
Onion Fingerlings

You'll never be able to eat just one!

MAKES 6 SERVINGS

INGREDIENTS

2 pounds
fingerling potatoes

3 tablespoons vegetable
oil

1 envelope
onion soup mix

salt and pepper

TOOLS

cutting board

sharp knife

measuring spoons

large mixing bowl

pasta server

baking sheet

spatula

oven mitts

1. Preheat the oven to 450 **degrees.** Cut the potatoes in half lengthwise

2. Put the potatoes, oil, and onion soup mix in a large bowl. Mix until the potatoes are evenly coated. Add salt and pepper to taste.

3. Arrange the potatoes on a baking sheet. Bake for 20 minutes. Turn the potatoes over with a spatula. Bake for 20 more minutes.

SAVORY
Potato-Bacon Salad

A creamy dish ideal for picnics, potlucks, and parties!

MAKES 6 SERVINGS

INGREDIENTS

2½ pounds
red potatoes

1 cup sour cream

½ cup mayonnaise

½ bunch green onions,
chopped

1 cup cheddar cheese,
grated

1 tablespoon
real bacon bits

TOOLS

large pot

pot holders

fork

strainer

large mixing bowl

spoon

cutting board

sharp knife

measuring cups

measuring spoons

mixing spoon

1. Place the whole potatoes in a pot of water. Bring it to a boil. Boil the potatoes for 10 minutes, or until you can poke a fork into them easily. Drain the water and set the potatoes aside. Let the potatoes cool completely.

2. Put the sour cream, mayonnaise, half of the chopped onions, half of the cheese, and half of the bacon bits in a large bowl. Mix well.

3. Cut the cooled potatoes into cubes.

4. Gently stir the potatoes into the sour cream mixture. Be careful not to mash them! Sprinkle the remaining cheese, onions, and bacon bits over the salad.

1

2

3

4

CHEDDAR
Potato Cakes

These cakes are corny, cheesy, and delicious!

MAKES 8 SMALL CAKES

INGREDIENTS

3 yellow potatoes, peeled

2 tablespoons butter

¼ cup milk

salt and pepper

½ teaspoon thyme

½ cup cheddar cheese, shredded

½ cup canned corn, drained

1 egg

½ teaspoon sugar

olive oil

TOOLS

cutting board

sharp knife

fork

medium pot

strainer

pot holders

measuring cups & spoons

mixing spoon

paper towels

peeler

can opener

plate

non-stick frying pan

spatula

① Fill a medium pot with water. Add a dash of salt. Bring it to a boil. While it is heating, chop the potatoes into 1-inch (2.5 cm) cubes. Add the potatoes to the boiling water. Cook for 10 to 15 minutes, or until potatoes are tender. Drain the water and return the potatoes to the pot.

② Add the butter, milk, and thyme. Add salt and pepper to taste. Mash thoroughly with a fork. Add the cheese, corn, egg, and sugar. Mix well.

③ Use your hands to form the mixture into eight round, flat cakes.

④ Put a paper towel on a plate. Heat ½ tablespoon oil in a non-stick frying pan over medium heat. Fry four potato cakes for about 5 minutes on each side. Put them on the plate. Put another ½ tablespoon of oil in the pan. Fry the other four cakes the same way. Serve warm.

TOMATOES

There are more than 7,000 kinds of tomatoes. Each looks, tastes, and grows differently. Most tomatoes are red. But some are yellow, orange, purple, green, or even white. They come in different shapes and sizes too.

Many tomatoes were created to grow well on patios. The plants don't get too big, but they produce a lot of tomatoes!

Cherry tomatoes are a popular patio tomato. But the recipes in this book work best with bigger tomatoes. So pick your favorite mid-size patio tomato, and let's get started!

TYPES OF TOMATOES

CHERRY

BEEFSTEAK

EARLY GIRL

BRANDYWINE HEIRLOOM

ROMA

LET'S GET
GROWING

In this section, you'll learn how to grow tomatoes in a **container** garden. With container gardens, you have more control over things such as light and temperature. But keep in mind that tomatoes grow differently in every climate.

When to Plant

Go online to find out the average date of the last frost in your area. Plant your **seedling** about one week after this date.

The Right Conditions

Sunlight
Tomato plants need six to eight hours of sunlight a day.

Temperature
*Tomatoes like the daytime temperature to be between 70 and 80 **degrees**. If it gets too cold, bring your tomato plants inside.*

Pests and Weeds
Be earth-friendly! Soap and water sprays keep pests away. White vinegar is a great weed killer.

Shade
Put your container in a location that gets some natural shade. Or bring it inside if it gets too hot.

The Right Soil
*Fertile, well-draining soil is a must! Also, make sure there is plenty of **nitrogen** in the soil when you plant your seedling.*

PLANT YOUR
SEEDLING

① **②** **③**

MATERIALS NEEDED

5 gallon container with drainage holes

soil

tomato seedling

tomato stake

mulch

water

trowel

① Fill your **container** three-quarters full of soil. Break up the soil so it is loose. Make a hole in the center.

② Carefully remove the **seedling** from its container. Set it in the hole. Arrange the soil around the plant so it is supported.

③ You may need to stake your plant. Put the stake in the soil near the seedling. Make sure the bottom of the stake hits the bottom of the container.

④ Add **mulch** around the seedling. Then water the plant thoroughly.

Watering

The trick is to water tomatoes heavily but not too often. Let the soil dry out between each watering. Always water your plants in the morning. Direct the water at the base of the plant. Try not to get the leaves wet.

Mulching

Using **mulch** will lock in moisture. It also keeps water and soil from splashing up onto the leaves.

GROWTH

Fertilizing

Tomato plants should be **fertilized** every 10 days until they start blooming. Feed them every two weeks while they are blooming. Stop fertilizing when tomatoes start to form.

Staking & Pruning

If you are growing a staked tomato, you will need to tie it to the stake. Do this when the plant starts to fall over. Remove lower leaves when the plant is small. After that, remove any new stems that start growing. This helps the main stem grow better.

STAKE your plant if it starts to fall over. Tie it to the stake with string or cloth.

HARVEST when the tomatoes reach their full color and are soft to the touch.

125

HARVESTING

TOMATOES

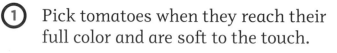

(1) Pick tomatoes when they reach their full color and are soft to the touch.

(2) Wash and dry the tomatoes. They'll keep at room temperature for about a week. Store them in the refrigerator if you're not going to use them right away. Or learn how to can them!

(3) Tomatoes can't ripen when the temperature is below 60 **degrees**. Bring the green tomatoes inside. Store them in a brown paper bag. The warmth in the bag will cause the tomatoes to ripen.

Tomato Q&A

QUESTIONS & ANSWERS

How Long Will it Take?

It depends on the sun, temperature, and type of tomato. Generally, **seedlings** need 60 to 90 days to grow ripe tomatoes.

Why are there black spots on my leaves? Or on my tomatoes?

These spots can be caused by several kinds of **fungi** and bacteria. Remove the **infected** leaves. If there are spots on a tomato, throw it away.

Why did my tomatoes split?

Changes in the weather or water supply can cause cracks in the tomatoes. Cracks are like stretch marks. The tomato grew too fast in too short of time.

Why is there a big black spot around the stem of my tomato?

This is caused by a lack of **calcium**. This happens when it doesn't get enough water. Plants **absorb** calcium along with water from the soil through their roots. If they don't get water, they can't get calcium.

PUCKER-UP

Orange Salsa

Kiss your old salsa recipe good-bye!

MAKES 2½ CUPS

INGREDIENTS

3 medium-sized tomatoes

½ medium-sized red onion

¼ cup fresh cilantro

1 tablespoon orange juice

1 teaspoon sugar

1 teaspoon salt

TOOLS

sharp knife

cutting board

measuring cups

medium mixing bowl

measuring spoons

mixing spoon

plastic wrap

1. Cut off the top and bottom of a tomato. Set the tomato on the cutting board. Place the tip of the knife in the center of the top of the tomato and cut down.

2. Gently pull the tomato open and set it down on the cutting board. Use the knife to cut away the insides of the tomato.

3. Repeat steps 1 and 2 with the other tomatoes.

4. Chop the tomato skins and red onion into small pieces. Finely chop the cilantro. Put the tomatoes, onions, and cilantro in a medium bowl.

5. Add the orange juice, sugar, and salt. Mix well. Cover the bowl with plastic wrap. Chill the salsa for 1 hour before serving.

1

2

4

5

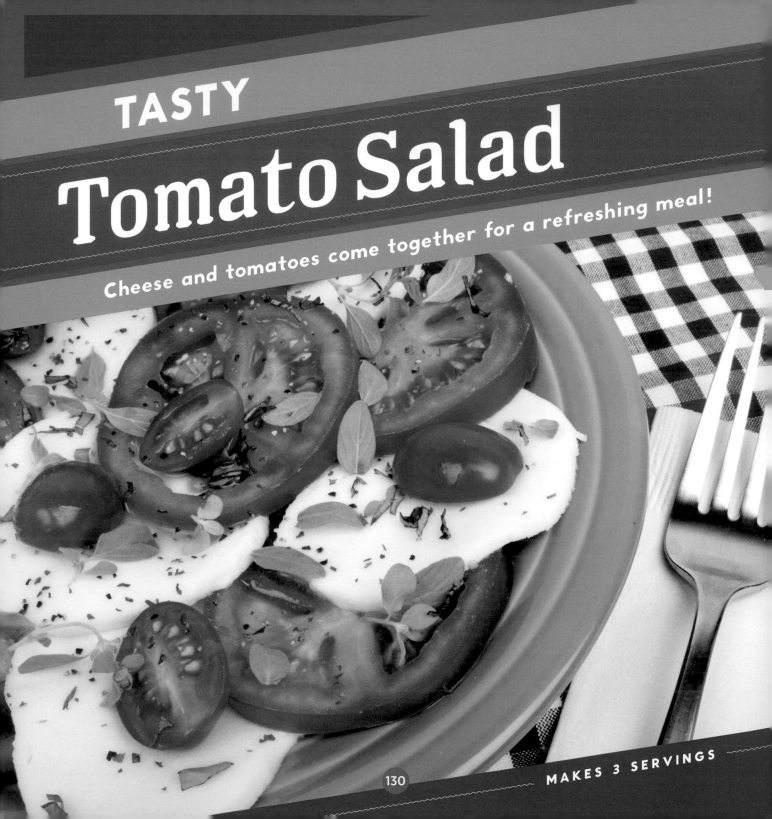

TASTY
Tomato Salad

Cheese and tomatoes come together for a refreshing meal!

MAKES 3 SERVINGS

INGREDIENTS

1 pound assorted tomatoes

6 to 7 slices fresh mozzarella cheese

1 teaspoon salt

1½ tablespoon red wine vinegar

½ teaspoon honey

¼ cup olive oil

2 sprigs marjoram

5 to 7 fresh basil leaves

TOOLS

sharp knife

cutting board

kitchen scissors

measuring spoons

medium mixing bowl

whisk

measuring cups

plate

spoon

① Slice the large tomatoes. Leave the smaller tomatoes whole, or cut them in half. Arrange the tomato and cheese slices on a plate.

② Put the the salt, vinegar, and honey in a medium bowl. Whisk until the salt **dissolves**. Then whisk in the olive oil. Drizzle the dressing over the tomatoes and mozzarella.

③ Strip the marjoram leaves from the stems. Add them to the salad. Use kitchen scissors cut up the basil leaves. Sprinkle the pieces over the salad. Add salt to taste.

1

2

3

CRISPY
Caprese Melt

Your favorite salad is now a sandwich!

MAKES 1 SANDWICH

INGREDIENTS

2 slices sourdough bread

½ tablespoon olive oil

6 fresh basil leaves

1 medium-sized tomato, sliced ¼ inch thick

1 ounce fresh mozzarella cheese, sliced ¼ inch thick

salt and pepper

TOOLS

cutting board

sharp knife

measuring spoons

basting brush

baking sheet

oven mitts

spatula

1. **Adjust** an oven rack so it is six inches from the top. Set the oven to broil. Brush one side of a bread slice with olive oil. Place it oil side down on a baking sheet.

2. Arrange the basil leaves, tomato slices, and mozzarella slices on the bread. Sprinkle lightly with salt and pepper.

3. Put the other bread slice on top. Brush it with olive oil. Broil the **sandwich** for 1 minute. Remove it from the oven. Turn the sandwich over with a spatula.

4. Put it back in the oven. Broil for 1 to 2 more minutes. The bread should be golden brown, and the cheese should be slightly melted. Slice the sandwich in half and serve immediately.

133

FRESH
Tomato Pasta

Enjoy the contrast of cool tomatoes and warm pasta!

MAKES 4 TO 6 SERVINGS

INGREDIENTS

1 pound fettuccine pasta

4 to 6 tomatoes, chopped

5 tablespoons olive oil

2 teaspoons lemon juice

⅓ cup fresh basil, chopped

salt and pepper

½ cup Parmesan cheese, grated

TOOLS

large pot

measuring spoons

measuring cups

cutting board

sharp knife

large mixing bowl

mixing spoon

strainer

pasta server

pot holders

① Cook the fettuccine according to the instructions on the package.

② Put the tomatoes, olive oil, lemon juice, and basil in a large bowl. Add salt and pepper to taste. Mix gently.

③ Drain the pasta when it is done. Put it in the bowl with the tomato mixture. Toss to mix. Sprinkle the Parmesan cheese on top. Serve immediately.

To Taste?

Sometimes a recipe says to add an ingredient "to taste." That means you decide how much to add! Start small. You can always add more later. It's harder to remove something than it is to add more!

BRILLIANT

Bruschetta

This simple, satisfying appetizer will go fast!

INGREDIENTS

12 baguette slices,
½ inch thick

olive oil

salt

3 to 4 medium tomatoes,
finely chopped

2 teaspoons fresh basil,
finely chopped

pepper

1 garlic clove, halved

½ cup mozzerella cheese,
grated

TOOLS

cutting board

bread knife

measuring cups

basting brush

baking sheet

measuring spoons

mixing bowl

mixing spoon

oven mitts

sharp knife

1. Set the oven to broil. Brush both sides of each piece of bread with olive oil. Put the bread slices on a baking sheet. Sprinkle them lightly with salt.

2. Mix the tomatoes, basil, and 2 tablespoons of olive oil in a bowl. Add salt and pepper to taste. Set the bowl aside.

3. Broil the bread for about 2 minutes. Turn the slices over. Broil for 2 more minutes. Watch the bread carefully. It should be browned but still soft in the center. Remove the bread from the oven. Let it cool slightly. Rub the halved garlic clove on each slice.

4. Put some of the tomato mixture on each bread slice. Add some mozzarella cheese to each piece. Put the baking sheet back in the oven for 1 minute. Then serve it immediately.

TOMATO
Pie in the Sky

Only garden fresh tomatoes will do!

MAKES 1 PIE

INGREDIENTS

4 medium-sized tomatoes, sliced

salt

9-inch uncooked pie shell

½ cup plus 3 tablespoons grated Parmesan cheese

½ cup green onion, chopped

¾ cup mayonnaise

1½ cups grated cheddar cheese

2 teaspoons cornstarch

¼ cup fresh basil leaves, chopped

pepper

TOOLS

cutting board

sharp knife

paper towels

measuring cups

pie pan

measuring spoons

medium mixing bowl

mixing spoon

oven mitts

1. Preheat the oven to 375 **degrees**. Put the tomato slices on paper towels. Sprinkle them with salt. Let them stand 10 minutes.

2. Put the uncooked pie shell in a pie pan. Sprinkle it with 3 tablespoons Parmesan cheese. Arrange the tomatoes and green onions in the pie shell.

3. Put the mayonnaise, cheddar cheese, ⅓ cup Parmesan cheese, cornstarch, and basil in a medium mixing bowl. Add salt and pepper to taste. Mix well.

4. Gently place spoonfuls of the mayonnaise mixture on the tomatoes. Carefully spread the mixture over the pie.

5. Sprinkle the remaining Parmesan cheese over the top. Bake for 30 to 40 minutes. The pie crust and mayonnaise mixture should be golden brown.

139

1

2

3

5

Glossary

ABSORB – to soak up or take in.

ADJUST – to change something slightly.

ALLERGY – sickness caused by touching, breathing, or eating certain things.

ALTERNATE – to change back and forth from one to the other.

BLIGHT – a sickness that kills plants.

CALCIUM – a soft, white element that most plants and animals need to be healthy.

CITRUS – a fruit such as an orange, lemon, or lime that has a thick skin and a juicy pulp.

COMPOST – a mixture of natural materials, such as food scraps and lawn clippings, that can turn into fertilizer over time.

CONSISTENT – always done the same way.

CONTAINER – something that other things can be put into.

CULTIVATE – to grow plants or crops.

CYLINDER – a solid shape with two parallel circles bound by a curved surface. A soda can is a cylinder.

DAMAGE – to cause harm or hurt to someone or something.

DEGREE – the unit used to measure temperature.

DENTAL – having to do with teeth.

DEVELOP – to grow or change over time.

DISSOLVE – to mix with a liquid so that it becomes part of the liquid.

DISTURB – to disorder or rearrange.

DRIZZLE – to pour in a thin stream.

EMERGENCY – a sudden, unexpected, dangerous situation that requires immediate attention.

ENVIRONMENT – nature and everything in it, such as the land, sea, and air.

FERTILIZE – to add something to the soil to make plants grow better.

FERTILIZER – something used to make plants grow better in soil.

FISH EMULSION – a fertilizer made from liquid left over during fish oil production.

FUNGUS – an organism, such as mold or mildew, that grows on rotting plants. The plural of fungus is fungi.

GARNISH – to decorate with small amounts of food.

GERMINATE – to begin to grow from a seed.

HERB – a scented plant used to flavor food or make medicine.

INFECTED – to have a disease caused by bacteria or other germs.

OAM – loose soil that has clay nd sand in it.

ATURE – to finish growing or eveloping.

ULCH – something, such as traw or wood chips, spread over he ground to protect plants.

ITROGEN – a gas that is in all ving things and makes up most f the earth's atmosphere.

UTRIENT – something that helps ving things grow. Vitamins, inerals, and proteins are utrients.

INCH – the amount you can hold etween your thumb and one nger.

ECOMMEND – to suggest or dvise.

SANDWICH – two pieces of bread with a filling, such as meat, cheese, or peanut butter, between them.

SCRUB – to clean by rubbing hard.

SEEDLING – a young plant that grew from a seed.

SHAMPOO – a special soap used to clean hair.

SOAK – to leave something in a liquid for a while.

SOLUBLE – able to dissolve in liquid.

SOW – to put seeds on or in soil so they will grow.

SPROUT – 1. to begin to grow. 2. a new plant growing from a seed.

TOASTED – cooked until it is dry and brown.

TRANSPORTATION – the act of moving people and things.

TRELLIS – a support made of crossed pieces of wood.

VARIETY – different types of one thing.

WATERLOGGED – completely full of water.

Web Sites

To learn more about growing and cooking food, visit ABDO Publishing Company on the World Wide Web at www.abdopublishing.com. Web sites about creative ways for kids to grow and cook food are featured on our Book Links page. These links are routinely monitored and updated to provide the most current information available.

Index